The Fascinating World Of Cotton, Threads & Spools
By
Alex Askaroff

The Fascinating World Of
Cotton,
Threads & Spools
By
Alex Askaroff

www.sewalot.com

The rights of Alex Askaroff as author of this work have been asserted by him in accordance with the Copyright, Designs and Patents Act.
©

For other publications
by
Alex Askaroff
Visit Amazon.

This is no masterpiece. It's more a self-published labour of love from someone who has spent a lifetime in the sewing trade and a million hours gathering facts for you. Many have been from fellow enthusiasts from around the world. I thank you all.

Why write these books? Easy, I find the world of sewing fascinating and I often feel that if I don't get it all down it will be lost forever. Beware! From my vast profits of around tuppence a book I'll invest in a new set of glasses from the Pound Shop and carry on scribbling!

With Eight No1 New Releases on Amazon, I must be getting something right!

Please forgive any inaccuracies, some of my work is legend and word of mouth falling down through the generations. Also watch out for my spelling, United Kingdom English, and please do enjoy it in the same spirit that it was written.

Alex Askaroff

Contents

Ever Wondered How Old Cotton Is?.........8

The Cotton Gin 1793..........................13

So How Long Have Sewing Threads Been Around?.......................................18

The First Needles............................22

Where Did The Needle Industry First Boom In England?................................25

Why Did Thread Manufacturing Start In Britain?.......................................28

Enter The Bogeyman.........................30

Substitute......................................35

Joseph Marie Jacquard......................37

1812..41

Paisley..42

Wind The Bobbin Up......................43

Clark & Co, Anchor Mills, Paisley.........45

The Invention Of Wooden Cotton Spools.48

Cotton Reels, Penny A Bucket!
The Paisley Cotton Reel Cart..............52

Boom & Bust...............................53

Mahatma Gandhi............................54

Master Bobbin Maker.......................55

The Bobbin Borer..........................55

The End Of The Wooden Bobbin...........57

Cotton Mills & Factories Act................59

Pop Goes The Weasel.......................61

Sewing Machines Are Coming!...............62

The Spool Cotton Company..................69
Coats & Clark

Dewhurst Sylko History......................70

English Cotton Company & British Sewing Cotton Company..............................73

Barbour Campbell Threads Ltd.............75

The American Civil War & The Cotton Shortage! 'Linenopolis'......................77

Dundee 'Cottonopolis'......................78

To Stretch Or Not To Stretch. That Is The Question........................79

When Did Polyester Thread Come Into General Use?..81

Ever Wondered How Old Cotton Is?

I have loved writing this booklet. I've spent 30 years gathering the most weird and wonderful facts about anything to do with fabrics, needles, threads and so much more, from all over the world.

I thought we could start our rollercoaster journey with cotton. It's everywhere, all around us. Even as I write someone will be rolling around in it, or stuffing a cotton bud down their ear canal (against doctor's orders). It is easy to imagine our ancestors thousands of years ago, walking along foraging for food, and coming across wild cotton.

They would have rolled it between their fingers and thought, 'now this could be useful', or maybe just 'ug, ug'. Either way they could have put it over their ears when the cold wind blows, in their footwear when winter drew close, padded their hide skins with it, cleaned themselves with it, even stored food in it.

Cotton has a thousand uses, but how long was it before one of our ancestors rolled it into lengths and roughly wove it together to form a pad or a piece of fabric?

At some point in our evolution pads of rough threads and fibre were jabbed and stabbed with barbed rough bone and wooden needles. This snagging together of fibres produced the first ever basic fabric, thousands of years before looms.

Amazingly we still use the same stuff today. We now call this basic fabric—felt. More of that later.

And then how long before our ancestors teased and twisted fibres from cotton or other plants into threads and wove it into fabric? The history of cotton and fabric is really the history of the Human Race.

We know that our earliest ancestors used animal skins, cotton, hemp and hessian to cover themselves and, as new archaeological evidence comes to light, it is showing us that even as far back as 80,000 years ago humans had covered their bodies. We may find that it goes even further back! So let us look more at this fabulous natural fibre.

Natural cotton has so many wonderful qualities that humans have used it for thousands of years.

Scientists in Mexico found pieces of fabric made from cotton cloth that were at least 7,000 years old. They also found that the cotton all those years ago was very similar to that grown today.

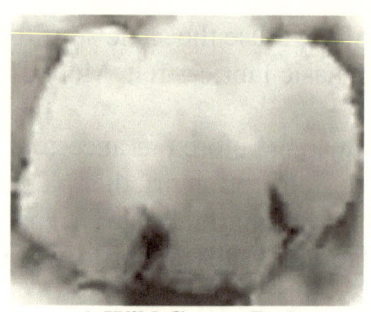

A Wild Cotton Bud

Amazingly, discoveries have shown that in Pakistan, cotton was being woven into cloth and regularly worn as a fabric over 5,000 years ago. However that's not the oldest!

Egyptian cotton has always been at the very top of quality cotton fabrics. Cleopatra wore the finest cotton grown in Egypt's Nile Valley, probably not while soaking in asses milk though!

Cotton is a member of the mallow family and was first grown commercially in Asia, Africa and Latin America. Cotton is a tough plant that loves a hot climate. In Peru, the Incas had grown cotton, as had the Mayans in Mexico, from about 5,000BC.

The first spinning wheel was thought to have originated in India about 500 years before Jesus was born. From that point on in history the first woven fabric was available to all who could afford it.

Single spun threads in various forms soon followed. That allowed these wonderful fabrics to be joined. Arab merchants apparently brought cotton to trade commercially in Europe as late as 800Ad.

However by the 1450's, cotton was known throughout the world. When Columbus bumped into a big lump of land and called it America in 1492, he found cotton cultivation already well established.

Cotton seeds are believed to have been planted in Florida around 1556 and in Virginia by 1607. By 1616, colonists were growing cotton along the James River in Virginia.

Cotton was first spun on industrial machinery in England in 1730 and we will be looking at that in more detail. Cotton later played an important part in the American Civil War as it was a precious resource. A little more about that later too. Everything changed when a Massachusetts man, Eli Whitney, secured a patent on a cotton gin in 1793.

Interestingly patent records show that the first cotton gin could actually have been built by a chap called Noah Homes two years before Whitney's patent.

How are you liking the blasts of fun facts so far? Don't worry by the end you'll know enough to enter the local pub quiz!

Wild cotton has not changed much in millennia and would have been a godsend to our early ancestors

The Cotton Gin 1793

The cotton gin, where we get the abbreviation of en--gine, could work 10 times faster than hand. With the arrival of the cotton gin our modern world arrived.

The mechanised gin, not the liquid stuff boys, made it possible to supply large quantities of cotton fibre to the ever-expanding textile industry.

That in turn made it possible to obtain cheaper clothing. Now we could all wear different clothes instead of the same scruffy ones. Primark was still a couple of centuries away, so clothes were costly.

Today, cotton is still one of the finest, natural and most durable of materials, even though it can crease like crazy. Cotton has replaced wool as a cash crop that many countries rely on. Turkey for instance produces high quality cotton and in 2016 grew and exported $453,000,000 of cotton yarn.

Current day cotton pickers in Mexico picking for the denim industry and a superb old cotton advert.

By the 1850's cotton was easily available at almost any corner store and sold by hundreds of different suppliers to countless retailers.

However it was not just cotton that was on the rise. Linen thread was durable and washable and had been used for a thousand things. With modern industrial methods it was now available for fine hand sewing and even sewing machines when clever old Elias Howe made his first machine in 1846.

Campbell's Irish linen thread was made in Belfast.

Campbell's sewing machine thread was linen not cotton but worked well in thicker fabrics. I talk a little more about Campbell's later.

James Hargreave's invention of The Spinning Jenny in 1764, had already changed everything. It sped up the process of cotton thread manufacture by eight times that of a traditional spinning wheel. Although the Lancashire weaver's invention revolutionised the textile industry, he never prospered from it.

This improvement was basically a response to keep up with John Kay's Flying Shuttle of 1733, which had sped up cloth manufacture. That in turn had increased yarn and thread demand from the weavers as they were doubling their productivity with modern machinery.

In some factories today the shuttles used in weaving have been replaced with computer controlled jets of air. They blast threads through the loom from spools holding 250km of thread each!

You can just make out the white spools of thread on this Spinning Jenny near the bottom. From this slow start you can see how the bobbins later evolved into the small thread spools that we know today.

The Spinning Jenny could now supply the ever increasing demand for cheaper thread. The Spinning Mule, invented by Samuel Crompton in 1779, spun fibres into yarn and thread even faster.

It was similar types of machines to these that spun the cotton threads onto the first small cotton spools for hand sewing and later for sewing machine use. And so the wooden cotton reel was born, yippee. Much more about the cotton reel later in my story.

With mass production in the fabric industry, materials became much cheaper. For the first time it wasn't just the wealthy, but the rest of us too, who could dress a little better. Maybe we could even have a separate suit for Sunday church! Mass production of fabric and threads had changed our world forever.

Well, now that we have touched on fabric and threads let's look a little closer at what holds all our stuff together.

So How Long Have Sewing Threads Been Around?

The answer is almost as long as humans have walked on two legs. Far longer than felt and fabric.

The first threads would have been little more than thin leather, animal tendons, sinew or twine, mainly used to stitch animal hides together.

We know that humans were grinding seeds over 100,000 years ago and it's pretty certain they were also using threads at a similar time. Animal hides used by humans for protection probably date from the same period. These 'all natural' materials rotted back into the soil so archaeologists almost never turn any up.

Otzi the Iceman, discovered frozen in the Otztaler Alps in 1991 showed just how advanced humans were 5,300 years ago. His leather and fur garments were beautifully hand stitched with animal sinews. The tears, which he probably repaired himself, were done with roughly twisted grasses. The murder of the Neolithic hunter gave us a rare window into the past. Even the Bronze Age had to be re-dated due to his weapons. From Otzi's frozen corpse (with the arrow head still in his back) we learnt more about our distant relatives than ever before.

Many ancient tribes knew which local plant or tree gave the best thread such as honeysuckle, reed and cactus. In Europe, wild clematis (Old Man's Beard) was used for millennia as twine, it has amazing strength. The list of twines and rough threads from animals and plants is endless. The fine roots of the spruce tree were used for threads, as was cedar. Birch bark was used in place of leather for baskets and stitched with dampened willow root.

The first human made fabrics were not woven but more similar to compacted fibres from cotton or any 'fluffly fibre' producing plant, tree or animal.

Compacting this 'fluff' produced felt. Rough needles (from wood or bone) jabbed through these fibres and joined them. Soaking and compressing the fibre then produced our first human fabrics. These could then be hand-stitched to form clothes and coverings.

It wasn't until the late 18th Century that mass produced wooden spools started to appear. Wooden cotton spools really took off from around 1820.

Amazingly felt is still produced in much the same way today (although on an industrial scale). Rows of barbed needles jump up and down between fibres, joining them as each fibre is pulled and tugged into felt before being compressed into fabric.

From Costa Rica to the Philippines, Abaca or Manila hemp was grown for fibre, thread, rope and later paper.

The Yucca plant, native to the Americas, has a wonderful gift, its sword shaped leaves end in a ferocious point. If you peel the point away carefully, a thread comes with it. That was used as a needle and thread. Our early ancestors knew all about these gifts from nature.

I adore these old adverts.

As the centuries went by we learnt more advanced ways how to fashion natural materials for our own use. We learnt to twist wool, silk, linen, cotton and many more, into fine threads.

The Chinese perfected the almost magical production and weaving of silk, mainly from the Mulberry moth silk worms, but from many other sources such as oysters, mussels, and even spiders!

India was close behind, after traded silk from China was used by the ruling elite. It didn't take them long to figure out how to make it themselves. Some legends tell that, at the risk of death, two monks smuggled silkworms from China to Istanbul along the Silk Road around 550AD.

However the secret escaped from China, by the 18th Century, the South East Asian countries had become the second largest silk producers in the world. They had perfected how to obtain a 1,000 metre strand of silk thread from a single silk worm cocoon! Now how crazy it that! Mind you they boil the little critter inside first!

As I mentioned earlier, the Egyptians had mastered the manufacture of linen and cotton (which they embalmed their loved ones with for eternity).

Finally, in our modern world, we mastered the manufacture of nylon, polyester and other synthetic threads. Amazingly, fabric and threads are always inextricably entwined with the story of our human evolution.

The First Needles

Of course if you are going to join any fabric or animal skin you are going to need a needle. The first needles or bodkins used to sew thread were animal bone, flint and wood. Later bronze and eventually steel so fine that they could pierce the most delicate silk without a mark.

Around 200,000 years ago, as humanoid migration moved northward from Africa into the colder climes of what we now call Europe, flint and bone ruled supreme as tools. The first needles discovered in Britain have been dated to around 10,000 years old and were animal bone. However there is no doubt there were needles here long before that. They have just all rotted.

Interestingly, although very little fabric and thread has ever turned up, we do know that human civilisation was advanced enough 10,000 years ago to make bricks for building. If we were building structures then we were certainly making and mending clothes (in the more advanced parts of the world anyway).

The oldest fibres to be discovered were in the Republic of Georgia in 2009. The flax fibres were dated at over 34,000 years old. In Turkey ancient remains of wool rugs have been dated to 6,500 B.C.

By Biblical times fabric was well advanced and split into classes and wealth. The wealthiest wearing everything from cotton, linen, wool and silk down to the poorest in undyed cloth and animal skins. Oh there are so many fabric facts and so little paper! Actually paper can be made from cotton, linen, animal skins and even rags, so that's no excuse! I do hope you are enjoying our journey so far, exciting isn't it!

Now, back to our first needles. Animal bones were shaped and smoothed using flint tools to make beautifully sharp needles. A well knapped flint is as sharp as the sharpest chef's blade. Often the stomach lining of animals were used for thread. As well as being strong it was also elastic. It was cut into fine slithers using flints, dried and used very successfully for thousands of years. Even into more recent history 'cat gut' was used in surgery to stitch us up and also made the best violin strings! Wet leather strips are still used for knife handle covering and much more. As it dries, it shrinks and locks tight.

Our ancestors knew how to survive using what was all around them. We wouldn't be here otherwise! Even today you could go out and cut a thorn from a blackthorn or hawthorn bush and make a perfect needle that will pierce leather! Funnily they were also the first fishing hooks!

Holly was a favourite needle with sewers as it has supple strength and was ideal for smaller needles. Net makers used them right up until the 20th Century.

Don't you think these old adverts are amazing!

In fact I still know a couple of traditional net makers in Eastbourne who use wooden needles made from holly. It has remarkable abilities to keep its point and not break. While we are on needles I can just imagine what you are thinking!

Where Did The Needle Industry First Boom In England?

No you weren't thinking of that! Never mind, let's talk about it anyway. For centuries the centre of the needle industry, not just England but the entire world, was Redditch, Worcestershire, producing the best needles on the market such as Milward's and Able Morrall's.

The Forge Mill next to Bordesley Abbey, Redditch, still survives and is well worth a visit. Originally a needle mill, the museum provides a fascinating insight into the early working life of the industrial revolution. It is where children as young as four worked for a living! Charles Dickens was delighted to see upon his visit that the age of children working at the Redditch Mill had risen to six!

Actually it is a fascinating point to raise. Some mill owners became fabulously wealthy and wasted money like water. Others, like Titus Salts and Robert Owen became the social reformers of their day. They built housing for their workers, improved living standards and much more. Robert Owen is even said to have started the first Co-Operative with his shops providing everything for the workers at a fair price.

Their fairness and moral reforms changed our world for the better and it was all due to textiles. Importantly they realised that happy workers were good workers. Mind you Robert still allowed children of ten to work in his Lanark mills (they could do evening school though).

The Forge Needle Museum is a great day out and a mass of information.

The Redditch needle industry kept the secret of fine needle making closely guarded. Punishment from the mill owners was so draconian that no one dared reveal the secrets of fine needle making. I was told that the fines could be as high as £15,000. That was a whole lifetime's earnings!

The closely guarded secret turned out to be amazingly simple. It was the endless grinding and polishing of the needles with fine grinding powders which produced their unbeatable needles. The water powered machinery proved so successful that it was used for generations and can still be seen working today. Don't worry I didn't get fined for passing on the secret!

Now that we have talked about fabric and needles let's actually look at where thread production started in Britain.

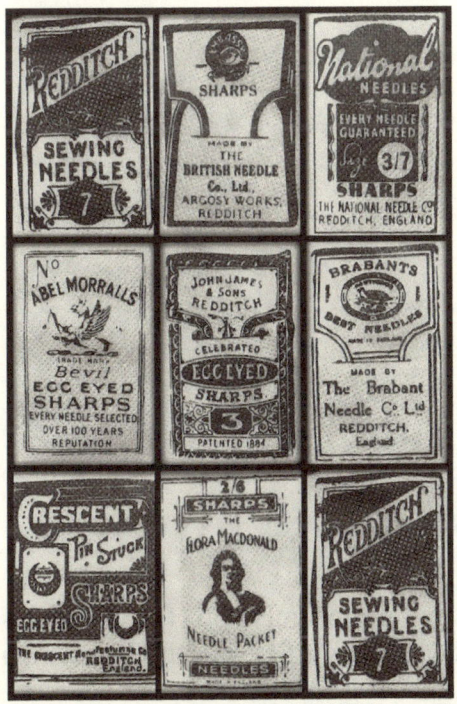

The Forge Needle Museum, Needle Mill Lane, Redditch.

Why Did Thread Manufacturing Start In Britain?

Firstly we must just mention Henna Wilkinson from Rhode Island, USA. She was the first American woman to ever gain a patent in her country. In 1793 Henna was awarded a patent for a cotton sewing thread, which she had twisted on her spinning wheel. The thread did not sew that well but she did

The closely guarded secret turned out to be amazingly simple. It was the endless grinding and polishing of the needles with fine grinding powders which produced their unbeatable needles. The water powered machinery proved so successful that it was used for generations and can still be seen working today. Don't worry I didn't get fined for passing on the secret!

Now that we have talked about fabric and needles let's actually look at where thread production started in Britain.

The Forge Needle Museum, Needle Mill Lane, Redditch.

Why Did Thread Manufacturing Start In Britain?

Firstly we must just mention Henna Wilkinson from Rhode Island, USA. She was the first American woman to ever gain a patent in her country. In 1793 Henna was awarded a patent for a cotton sewing thread, which she had twisted on her spinning wheel. The thread did not sew that well but she did go down in history as the first inventor and first woman patent holder.

However the real invention of the first super sewing thread (which led from a single mill to one of the largest companies in the world) all started in Scotland in the early part of the 19th Century.

So now we know that Britain is where thread manufacturing flourished, you have to wonder why? Why did Britain become so huge in the thread industry? You will never guess the answer.

Birmingham & Redditch were the centre of the world needle industry for decades so it was little surprise thread manufacturing would boom in Britain too.

Enter The Bogeyman

In 1806, nasty Napoleon Bonaparte was on the warpath. This is where some say we get the name 'Bogeyman' originally coming from, (Bonaparte—Bonepart—Boney—Bogey—Bogeyman).

Children were scared into behaving with tales of 'the Bogeyman' who would come over the water to take any naughty children away. What horrible parents eh! However, these 'Bogey' stories were slightly based on real events of the period.

Napoleon had made a massive sea blockade around the coasts of Britain. This made trade almost impossible. Another big problem was that France was a huge silk supplier. Funny really, I don't even mention silk in my book title and yet it is completely entwined with the history of cotton and threads.

Silk was being used for so many things that it was taken for granted back in that period, from silk wallpaper to silk umbrellas, and most importantly for use as silk sewing thread.

Perivale Pure Silk Thread. Many old sewing baskets still contain a few reels of silk thread.

Smugglers and convoys did break through the blockades but the goods they got through were expensive. Also silk thread was way down the list, below alcohol, tea and other sought after commodities.

The defeat of Napoleon's fleet at Trafalgar left him embittered and out for vengeance. This stopped almost all but the most ardent trader from bringing goods to England. All ships were prey to the French fleet and manufacturing in Britain was suffering.

William Maddick
'Black Silk' Manufacturer
Primrose Street & Love Lane
Spitalfields
London
1821

Heminway silk threads. Each reel was a week's wage!

In turn the silk threads, which had been used for sewing, became scarce and incredibly expensive. An alternative needed to be found if manufacturing was not to collapse.

Jonas, James & Joseph Brooks
(Trading as United Threads since 1890)
Purveyors of the finest silk threads.
We employ over 1,000 workers
At our Meltham Silk Mills
Holme Valley
West Yorkshire

Incidentally, silk threads are highly collectible today and make a great display. Initially silk sewed better than cotton and had more flexibility. Another bonus to silk was that the shine reflected the fabric, so it matched better and became almost invisible.

However, there was a huge drawback, the cost. One reel of silk was as much as one weeks wages in 1820! Upper classes only I'm afraid, unless the odd reel happened to fall into the scullery maids pocket whilst spring cleaning!

As sewing machines became more and more common, Clark & Co took pains to advertise that their cotton was okay to use on the new-fangled machines.

With sewing silk becoming so scarce a few skilled smugglers managed to break through the blockades in the dead of night, (their vessels often painted matt black and set with black sails to slip silently into moonlit bays). Such was the demand that it is said that silk was smuggled from every major port in Europe.

Interestingly, unlike skeins of silk, fine Italian silk was often wrapped on straight wooden cards with wood end caps to stop it from unravelling. Then placed in partitioned packing boxes for travel.

Fine Italian silk was often supplied on cards like these.

Substitute

So, silk was hard to get and a crazy price. The sewing houses up and down the country were screaming for help. I mean what would happen if we could not join fabric together? Go back to hemp twine and cat gut! A thread substitute was needed to keep the sewing ladies of Britain supplied, the sooner the better.

Willimantic Linen Thread flourished while silk was scarce.

The cost of all threads rocketed as did tobacco and booze. Great years for the smugglers! Brandy for the parson and silk for the lady! Personally I would have missed my morning cup of tea the most.

Interestingly the main booming silk industry had originally found its way to Britain with the arrival of the Huguenots (and one of my first French ancestors) when they fled from persecution. Many focused themselves around the Brick Lane area of London.

Joseph Marie Jacquard

It was the Frenchman Joseph Marie Jacquard who had perfected the 'Jacquard Loom' using paper punch cards. He had perfected machinery the likes no other weaver had seen before. The weavers loom was that magic instrument that turned threads into cloth.

A skilled loom worker could make about two inches of silk fabric A DAY! The Jacquard Loom made 60 inches a day. His machine did the work of 30 workers!

Now for an even more astounding fact. As I write, there is one factory in Bangkok that can make, in just one morning, the equivalent silk cloth that was woven by a whole village in one year! Think about that because it really is a WOW fact.

Joseph Marie Jacquard 1752-1834

Interestingly, his use of punch cards (to automatically make his machines copy certain patterns and colours) was the very same technique used by the computer industry right up until the 1970s. Paper cards riddled with holes were used to encode computers before they became fully electronic. Who could have guessed where it all started!

I love this silk thread advert. How to catch your man on a Leap Year!

By 1851 Britain had over 100,000 silk weavers. Today as I write I believe there is only one fully working silk mill left which is open to the public in England at Whitchurch. Whitchurch Silk Mill is in Hampshire, though Derby Silk Mill and others may be open to the public once again in the near future.

A saying emerged around that time.

'We are all born Adam's children but silk makes the difference'. They still use a similar phrase in Savile Row today 'The clothes maketh the man'. It was originally attributed to William Shakespeare.

1812

However we are jumping ahead, stay with me now as we discover how Britain ended up as the centre of the cotton thread industry. It is 1812 and Britain is being blockaded by Napoleon. Silk, the best sewing thread available, has become a silly price even if you could find some.

Hanks of silk from China and Asia could not get to England and an alternative was needed, fast! Everything was being reused and recycled. Even old tarred ship ropes were teased apart and rewoven.

With no hanks and skeins of silk, business was suffering all over the country. Now we travel to Paisley in Scotland. In fact with jobs suffering in the capital many of the London silk weavers also travelled north in search of work, taking their silk weaving skills with them.

This migration of skill, and cheap labour, was one of the reasons mills later flourished in the north of the country. Hey ho, it's off to Paisley we go.

Paisley

A classic Paisley Shawl

Initially, local Paisley weavers, working from home, had found a market making and supplying the larger cities with woven shawls, a 'must have' item (and still popular today).

Weaving soon moved from the age old cottage industry at home to huge mills. Notice the children growing up around the looms.

One of the nation's favourite children's songs came from this period, Wind The Bobbin Up. There are many versions. It is the rhythm and the beat which allowed the children in the mills to get the bobbins wound properly.

Wind the bobbin up
Wind the bobbin up
Pull, pull, clap, clap, clap

Wind it back again
Wind it back again
Pull, pull, clap, clap, clap

Point to the ceiling
Point to the floor
Point to the window
Point to the door

Clap your hands together, one, two, three
Put your hands upon your knee
Wind the bobbin up
Wind the bobbin up
Pull, pull, clap, clap, clap

Wind it back again
Wind it back again
Pull, pull, clap, clap, clap

These cottage industries around Paisley needed regular supplies of threads and materials. Hemp, hessian, cotton and any silk was shipped into Paisley. It became a centre for hand woven goods.

Over 30,000 people were soon involved in a massive trade that had traditionally grown from a small cottage industry. But more was to follow. The factories were coming!

Coats Best Six Cord was strong enough not to break when sewing on sewing machines.

From the 1700s, Mills in Scotland were popping up like mushrooms on a damp August evening. By 1760 there were over 100 mills twisting linen thread to supply demand. The scene and place was set for the next event on our journey.

Clark & Co
Anchor Mills
Paisley

In 1812, James and Patrick Clark were running a mill supply business in Paisley. The business was suffering badly from the lack of supplies. Napoleon's economic sanctions were crippling a country used to its luxury goods.

Patrick Clark came to our rescue inventing a method too twist cotton threads together to produce an excellent sewing thread for most applications.

Patrick had been experimenting for years with different yarns for sewing thread. Flax proved too rough, wool to thick, Heddle twine to variable. However with cotton, Patrick Clark (sometimes referred to as Peter Clark) hit the nail on the head. He eventually worked out an entirely new method of twisting, treating and teasing cotton fibres into a fine sewing thread.

The best raw cotton fibre at the time was from America and some colonies of the Empire. Even though cotton could be recycled from used fabrics there was still a big shortage.

The Clark Family, already supplying other threads from their mills, started to supply the cotton sewing threads that old man Patrick had perfected.

The Clark Family were possibly the first business in the world to mass produce cotton threads for the sewing industry.

Clark's Stranded Cotton. Skeins of thread similar to these were how most thread was supplied before the invention of the spool. It is still popular today for hobbies like cross-stitch.

The Invention Of Wooden Cotton Spools

For most of history, cotton and other materials were hand woven for use in fabric manufacture. From the earliest civilisation right up until the 17th century things had not changed that much. But as I mentioned earlier the Spinning Jenny, and other machinery, changed all that.

With the mass production of threads for textiles, another invention came about that lasted right up until the 1960's. The mass production of wooden cotton reels or spools for sewing threads.

Within a few years from the 1820's wooden cotton reels were being mass produced all over the world. I believe from all my research that the very first commercially sold wooden cotton reels (that held the same lengths of thread) were produced by the Clark Family in Paisley.

The Clark family turned birch and other similar wood spools cut from the Scottish forests. The small wooden spools they designed were just for holding sewing thread. Basically they were a smaller wooden version of the spindle cones first used in the Spinning Jenny. The small wooden spool was a brand new design for the ever growing market.

Initially, for a small fee, you could have your thread colour wound onto the wooden spools. The spools had a deposit on them (initially half-a-penny) so when you ran out of thread you sent or took the spool back for a refill.

This was a stroke of marketing genius by the Clark Family, as most local people, finding how good the spools worked, regularly took them back to the factory for refills.

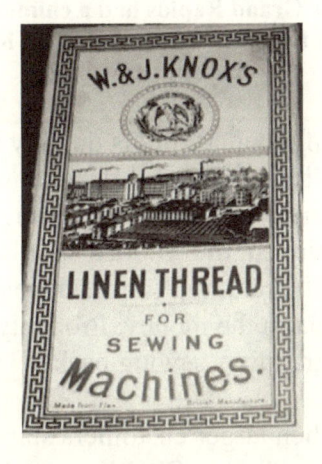

W J Knox's linen thread was made from flax in Kilbirnie, Scotland and direct competition to Clark's cotton thread. Its success lay in a special reverse twist in the linen thread that allowed it to stay strong and supple.

Clark's thread was wound onto the wooden reels with a spooling machine (some say invented by John Clark of Mile End Glasgow, though Barbour Thread also have a claim). Initially it was just local trade but as more and more spools were made, they spread wider afield.

Eventually wooden spools became the world standard method of thread storage. So, starting around the 1820's in Britain, cotton thread was stored for sale on specially fabricated wooden spools. The wooden cotton reel was here to stay. Well until plastic came along. I'll mention that later.

The Belding Corticelli Thread Co Belding, Michigan

The Belding Cortecelli Thread Company in Belding, Michigan, near Grand Rapids had a chimney stack so tall it could be seen for miles. I believe what is left of the mill is now protected.

The making of wooden spools quickly became automated. With industrial expansion worldwide, they consequently became far cheaper. Funnily, at first as I mentioned, the wooden spools from Clark's could be returned for the deposit. Kids would often claim the money. Probably with spools nicked from grannie's sewing basket!

It was only when larger customers started ordering cotton reels in bulk that Clark's started putting labels on the wooden cotton reels. That makes dating wooden reels far easier.

The first wooden reels came in all sorts of sizes. Here I am in 2021 with a standard reel and one with a mile of thread on it.

The first wooden cotton spools or reels from the 1820's were usually just plain unprinted Birch, Ash, or Sycamore woods, so pretty impossible to date. Also once any Tom, Dick or Harry saw the wooden reels of thread, they made them too. It must have been one of those 'slap the head' moments when everyone thought 'why didn't I think of that'.

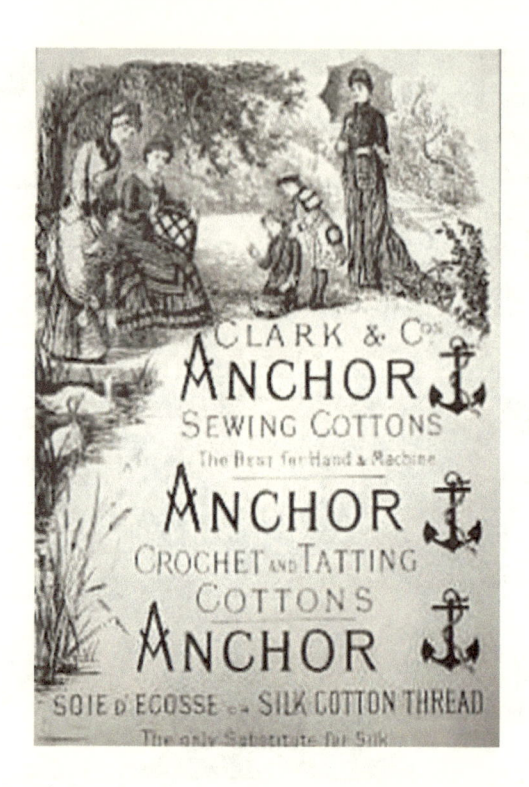

Crochet & Tatting Cottons became the ideal substitute for real silk and sewed well

Cotton Reels, Penny A Bucket! The Paisley Cotton Reel Cart

Mass production put an end to deposits on cotton reels. The price was soon included in the total cost of the thread and they became cheap enough to give away with the thread without a deposit.

I remember meeting a Paisley girl who as a child would hear the bell of the 'Paisley Cart' ringing along her street. Every Monday the horse drawn cart, containing all the broken and mis-formed or damaged wooden spools from the factories, were

sold for a penny-a-bucket to locals for fire kindling. When production was at its peak the chimney stacks belched out black smoke and the whole town took on the cloak of an industrial powerhouse.
Apparently the locals could always tell what colour thread was being made by the colour of the river. The excess dye stained the River Cart all the shades of the rainbow as it flowed down to the Clyde.

Boom & Bust

Great mills also grew in Cumbria, around the lakes, once again using Ash, Beech, Birch and more for the bobbins. All from carefully coppiced woods. These bobbin mills used the latest industrialised machinery to produce amazing amounts of wooden bobbins to supply the thread making mills.

Another amazing fact coming up. At their peak in the 1860's a skilled bobbin maker could turn over 3,000 bobbins a day and an average factory over 250,000 wooden cotton bobbins a week!

They fed the hungry northern mills with bobbins and the mill owners grew rich. Over 2,500 cotton mills in Britain produced around half the entire world's cotton in 1867! How crazy is that! One small island in the North Sea producing half of the entire world's cotton and we never even grew the stuff!

Cotton fabrics poured out on automated looms to feed the ever hungry consumer market. Mill owner James Bullough (1800-1868) became the first cotton millionaire, spending his wealth on grand houses and beautiful things.

James had made improvements to speed up the automation of the Lancashire Loom and reaped the rewards, becoming one of Queen Victoria's new 'elite' in her ever expanding Empire; only faltering for a time when cotton supplies dropped during the American Civil War.

Mahatma Gandhi

Much later Mahatma Gandhi also put his boot in during the 1920's. He called for a boycott of Lancashire fabric. He wanted to bring mass employment to his own country and saw the Lancashire Mills as a threat. The affect was devastating with mills dropping like flies, over twenty-a-year closing.

By the 1930's the boom time was over for the northern mills of Britain. Many countries around the world had started manufacturing their own fabrics, India and Japan leading the way.

Mahatma Gandhi was a passionate spinner, believing that he could bring back massive employment to India.

But once again we must step back and see how this early rapid growth went from a smouldering ember into a roaring fire. Let's look at the bobbin makers.

Master Bobbin Maker

As mechanisation flourished in the mid-19th Century bobbins became easier and cheaper to produce. The Master Bobbin Maker, using semi-automated machines, became such a high-speed craftsman that on a good day, he could produce thousands of wooden bobbins. Being paid piece work this allowed him a great wage and he often lived in one of the finer cottages in the area.

The Bobbin Borer

Bobbin boring was usually undertaken by women who were faster and more accurate than the men at the job. Once again it was piecework and the Cumbrian Mills kept the cotton industry well fed all over Britain, whether it was for small cotton reels for home sewing, industrial bobbins for factories or loom bobbins for cotton weaving.

Stott Park Bobbin Mill Museum is a brilliant place to visit. You get a real sense of the drama of working in a Victorian factory as they made countless wooden bobbins for the factories.

The End Of The Wooden Bobbin

By the 1950's plastic was coming online and the last of the big wooden bobbin factories slowly ground to a halt. Plastic became king until its persecution in the 21st Century. I wonder if wooden spools will return?

I believe the Stott Park Bobbin Mill, on the shores of Lake Windermere, is the last mill up in The Lake District that still shows how the early Victorian bobbins were made. Run by English Heritage, it should be on your list of places to visit.

Clark & Co Anchor Mills Paisley

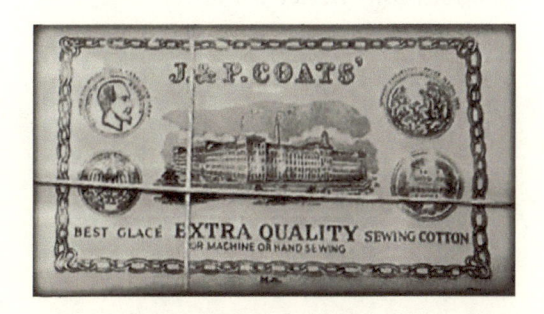

J & P Coats Best Glace Sewing Cotton

Now, back to our thread history after that very interesting diversion into wooden bobbins.

I believe that we also have James Coats from the same area of Scotland. James was from a family of weavers and seeing the success of Clark's, opened a factory near his home in 1826, Ferguslie Mill, Paisley, Scotland. He never looked back. In fact by the 1820's there were at least 15 mills manufacturing cotton just in Paisley!

After James Coats retirement in 1830 his son James (another James) and Peter Coats continued the Coats enterprise. From this point on all their threads were marked J & P Coats and so two of the biggest names in thread were established in Paisley and all originally because of the Bogey Man!

New Lanark Cotton Mills on the banks of the great River Clyde employed thousands of workers including 500 children from the age of six upwards!

The largest cotton mill in the country was a massive employer for the area. When Welshman Robert Owen took over the reins he strived to make working conditions better for all.

The New Lanark Cotton Mills look much the same today as they did 100 years ago.

Cotton Mills & Factories Act

In 1819, Sir Robert Peel introduced The Cotton Mills & Factories Act to regulate the use of children in the cotton mills and other industries.

It forbade children under the age of nine from working in the cotton mills. However, families tried to get around this law and children were taught to lie about their age to get work. It was a poorly enforced law as both the mill owners and workers families operated together to break it.

It is hard to judge life back then, to our standards today. Children would work on the farm as soon as they could lift a bucket and in the mills as soon as they could work safely amongst the machinery. In the small weaver's cottages and mills, nursery rhymes were sung to make it easier and more fun for the kids while working.

I wonder if you asked a child today if they would prefer to go to school or work on the farm what they would say. There is no doubt that when the whole family pulled together to survive everyone had more. That is much the way it must have worked since early human times.

Sylko's silken lustre crochet thread

Anyway, good, bad, or progress, here is one of the most famous nursery rhymes from that period that is still loved today, though few know it's hard reason for coming to life. The wording has changed over the last few years but the first part, which came to life in the weaver's cottages and mills of the Great Industrial North has not.

Pop Goes The Weasel

Firstly let me explain. In the cloth manufacturing industry the yarn winding instrument was called a weasel. To measure the amount of yarn wound onto the weasel there was a simple device which made a 'popping' sound at regular intervals. This 'popping' allowed the person counting to keep track of how much thread had been wound. Hence the term 'pop goes the weasel'.

There are many versions of the old rhyme but it is generally believed that it originated from the north of England. Here is one version from Skipton, circa 1830.

Half a pound of tuppeny rice,
Half a pound of treacle,
That's the way the money goes,
'Pop' goes the weasel.

A penny for a spool of thread,
A penny for a needle,
That's the way the money goes,
'Pop' goes the weasel.

Mummy taught me how to sew,
And how to count the cot-ton,
That's the way the mon-ey goes,
'Pop' goes the weasel.

An early advertising card showing Gulliver taking thread to the Lilliputians and showing them how strong it was.

Sewing Machines Are Coming!

With the invention of the sewing machine, threads had to change. Initially in 1846 Elias Howe had invented a sewing machine that worked but it was really Isaac Singer who changed the world with his amazing machine of 1851. As his machines spread across the world (and made him rich) a thread was needed that worked reliably on the machines.

Merrick Thread Co's
Best Sea Island Patent Shuttle Cotton,
Warranted 200 Yards
for Singer and other Sewing Machines

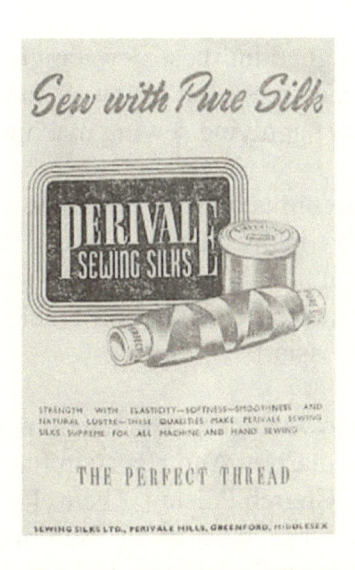

Perivale pure silk thread was king until the invention of high quality polyester threads that copied silks ability to give with the fabric, and its shine reflected the material into which it was sewn, making it almost invisible.

The race was on to produce a thread that did not mess up when used on a sewing engine or sewing machine. Many people don't realise how hard the thread has to work on a sewing machine. If you make a mark on the thread on your sewing machine about an inch above the needle then carefully sew a piece of fabric turning the machine by hand, you will notice that the thread travels through the needle eye, up and down, many times before it is eventually locked into the fabric.

The original two, three and four cord hand sewing thread was not strong enough for sewing machines and it unravelled as it sewed. This was a nightmare for the new sewing machine industry of the 1840's. However, George A Clark, one of the grandsons of the Clark dynasty, invented a six cord thread specially designed for these new-fangled gadgets. Other manufacturers soon followed and a huge industry grew supplying sewing machine thread.

One point of confusion with the Clark family was that there were many George Clark's. Family tradition has it that the Clark's eldest son was always called George! That didn't make my research any easier!

Our main man, George Clark, thread manufacturer and designer married Ann Henry in Paisley 12th Jun 1802 at Low Church Paisley. Their eldest son (you guessed it, George) born about 1823 married Catherine Dunlop Ballantyne, 13th Jun 1855 in Edinburgh. He is listed on the census of the period as manufacturer of 'sewed muslins'.

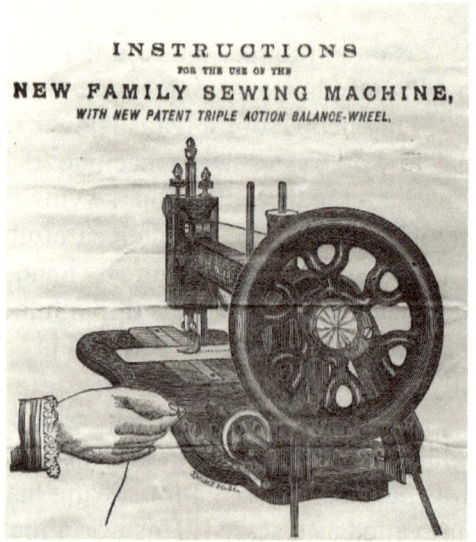

The first bestselling sewing machine on Planet Earth was the Singer model 12. It was in production from the American Civil war right up to 1901. It was essential that thread could be used on these new-fangled contraptions.

Cleverly George had somehow found a way to add a little elasticity to his reels of cotton thread (a closely guarded secret lost today). It allowed the thread to slide through the sewing machine guides with ease.

Until the invention of the superior polyester threads, Clark's cotton threads were simply the best available all around the world.

O N T Our New Thread for hand and machine sewing. But why 1812? There were no sewing machines then. Perhaps this much later advert was to show the world that Clark's were the first! A bit of creative advertising perhaps.

The six-cord soft thread sewed very well and helped the sewing machine industry flourish compared to the wiry old hand-sewing stuff. The new 'extra quality' thread sewed by hand or sewing machine!

One problem that was not cured until the thinner stronger polyester threads came along, was sewing very fine fabric. The thicker cotton knots (from the lockstitches) in the fine fabric (when the fabric was already tightly woven) caused puckering that could not be overcome. Besides that, it was a practical thread. Many clever designers incorporated this unavoidable 'puckering' in their designs.

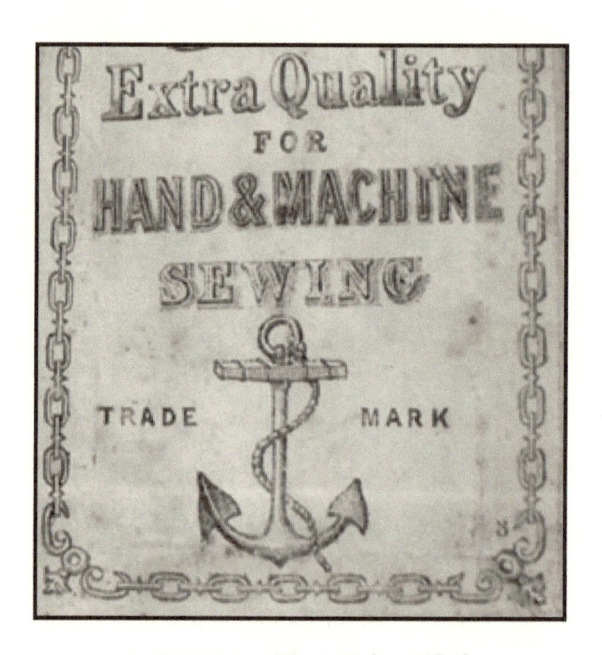

Clark sewing thread circa 1860

The new 'wonder' thread was clearly labelled. Each reel was marked with the initials "ONT" Our New Thread. Simple eh! I would love to find one of these reels as it would date it to around 1850.

By 1860 the Clark's factory at Paisley was booming. They won awards for their six cord threads at London and Brussels. They also won gold at the Exposition Universelle in Paris.

Clark & Co became the unrivalled sewing thread for machines and smoke from the great Anchor Mills Factory darkened the Paisley sky six days a week.

Anchor Mills, Paisley. Home of Clark & Co

Silk threads had been around years before Clark and Coats, so look carefully in your sewing box, you may have an ancient wrap or skein of silk thread in there.

1855 Clark's ONT, Our New Thread,
was specially designed for the new-fangled gadgets of the age called sewing machines. However they were careful to market the thread as suitable for old fashioned hand sewing as well.

Interestingly, wooden spools have recently started to become collectible and the values have been rising on the auction sites. What we once threw away without a second thought has become something to cherish. This book could be the start of many written by future experts and collectors.

The Spool Cotton Company
Coats & Clark

By the 1890's the two main Paisley thread companies joined and became one huge company. Coats & Clark became the Spool Cotton Company though both industries kept their separate identities when selling threads (to corner the expanding markets of the world). They traded separately as the Clark Thread Company and J & P Coats.

By the outbreak of The First World War, Coats had become one of the largest industrial companies in the entire world and all because of Napoleon!

In 1931 John B Clark was elected president of the combined companies. They expanded globally until 1952 when the companies merged completely becoming Coats & Clark Incorporated.

Coats & Clark eventually joined to become Coats & Clark Inc.

Dewhurst Sylko History

Dewhurst Three Shells Sylko thread.

The Dewhurst Cotton Company started with Thomas Dewhurst who bought a corn mill at Elslack, near Skipton, in 1789. He converted it into a cotton mill and spun cotton, using the river running by the factory to power his machines.

More mills followed as the business expanded, the most famous being Belle Vue Mills in Skipton, built by John Dewhurst in 1828.

From Belle Vue Mills, threads were shipped by canal across the country to docks and then exported across The Empire. The most important reason for the British Empire was the worldwide trade it allowed which was all centered on our small island.

Dewhurst Three Shells silk substitute thread from the Belle View Mills in Skipton. When silk became hard to get and expensive, a substitute was needed and Dewhurst made some superb silk substitutes in their Skipton mills.

John and Isaac Dewhurst, sons of Thomas Dewhurst, carried on the family business and became famous for their sewing cotton.

Dewhurst's enormous mill at Skipton, with its 225 ft Chimney, set the pace and time of the town with its 'mill buzzer' which roared out over the houses at set times each day.

The company perfected a wet twist cotton using three balanced cords. The thread was then 'gas shaved' before mercerisation to remove the fine whiskers of thread that made normal threads so fluffy. Sylko Three Shells thread earned a superb reputation and many reels survive to this day.

Right up until the 1950's Dewhurst's employed over 500 people in the Skipton area. However once again cheap imports and rising production costs slowly caused the decline of the business in Britain.

J & P Coats best six cord cotton in yards and meters for the export trade. Coats and Dewhurst were originally in direct competition.

English Cotton Company
&
British Sewing Cotton Company

Marketed under the Dewhurst Sylko brand, it eventually became part of the The English Cotton Company. An amalgamation of over 14 companies. In 1897 was headed by Algernon Dewhurst (John's Grandson).

Sylko, was available in over 500 shades and became internationally famous. Coats currently supply some Sylko branded threads.

It all gets a bit messy from here on, Dewhurst, part of the Ingham-Dewhurst-Illingworth group, was sucked up by Coats (Coats—Viyella) after English Sewing Cotton or the English Cotton Company or the British Sewing Cotton Company, sold out to Calico Printers (who then became Tootal in 1973). Told you it was confusing. All British manufacturing had to adapt to survive during this massive decline in manufacturing.

Coats & Clark were the largest thread manufactures in the world employing around 20,000 people in over 50 countries. In January of 2019 Spinrite acquired part of the North American Coats & Clark empire.

Here is a Sylko badge for Sylko mercerised cotton. The labels have a host of information from the Three Shells logo to the old Coats chain logo.

Incidentally Sylko is the name of my dog in my book The Magic Sewing Machine. A No1 new release. Amazon certified.

"Alex The Magic Sewing Machine is so wonderful that when my granddaughter stays, she won't go to bed unless I read this to her. Every night."

Barbour Campbell Threads Ltd

One interesting point with old threads is that the earliest reel of thread I have come across so far is a Barbour linen thread of 1784. Incidentally the same year that John Barbour (amazingly another Scotsman from Paisley) founded his business at The Lisburn Thread Mill, County Antrim, Ireland.

Barbour's home-spun Irish yarn gained a huge reputation for quality. For decades it was used for just about everything from stitching up humans on the operating tables to parachute cord. Barbour's Finest Cat Gut was in regular use in most hospitals.

Their huge Lisburn Mill was three stories high, set on 13 acres of land. The Barbour family built a village of homes, community hall, schools and shops for their workers. At their peak there were around two thousand workers in this mill alone.

Barbour thread mills also opened in New Jersey, America, and Manchester, England, also in Hamburg, Germany. Interestingly one of the wealthy heirs, Letisha Barbour bought a three mile island in the middle of the Susquehanna River in America. It later became the home of the notorious Three Mile Island Power Station.

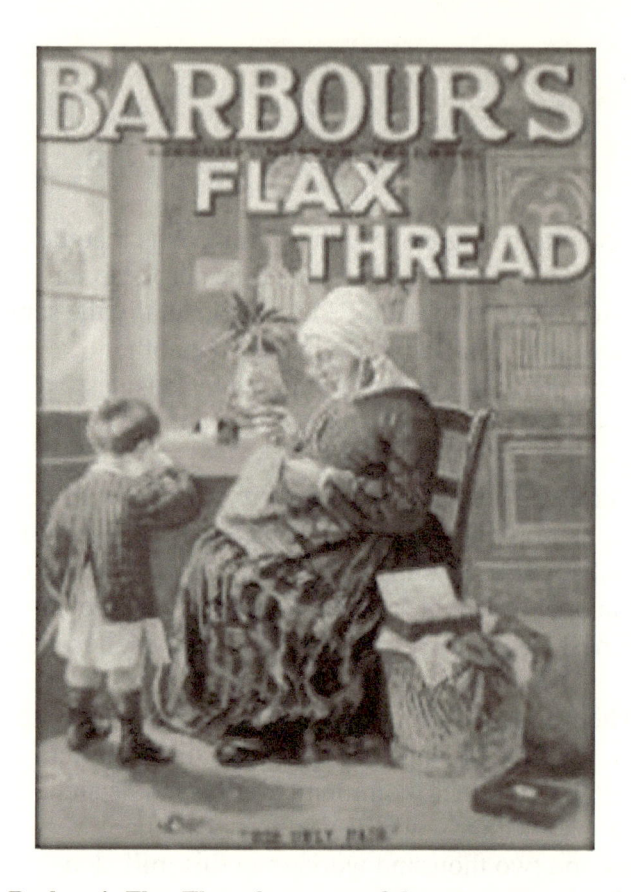

Barbour's Flax Thread was one of the strongest natural threads, being woven and twisted from the stalk of the flax plant. Many thanks to Caroline Harris for the advert.

The American Civil War
&
The Cotton Shortage!
'Linenopolis'

As I mentioned right at the start of our journey The American Civil war created a worldwide cotton shortage, but also opportunities.

In Ireland, linen production was already well established. Flax crops loved the cool wet conditions of Ireland and flourished there. Belfast factories were ideally situated to fill the sudden gap created by the civil war raging on the other side of the world in America.

Belfast became a boomtown doubling in size every few decades. During the Victorian Era, Belfast became known as 'Linenopolis' with some factories employing over 5,000 workers.

A few factories had over 1,000 looms powered by the latest steam engines. Belfast became the largest linen producers on Earth, producing material and threads for a hungry market starved of cotton. Interestingly, window cleaners tell me that an old linen cloth is still the best window cleaner.

Dundee 'Cottonopolis'

Scottish flax was also seen as the finest available in the 18th Century. The flax was normally harvested by gypsies who worked the cycles of the farming year, travelling from farm to farm as needed. From fruit picking to the flax harvest, gypsies travelled the width and breadth of Britain supplying the farmers with what they needed most, cheap labour.

The gypsies cut the stalks of the flax plant from which the fibre could be extracted to make canvas and other fabrics such as linen.

The farmers sold their flax to the weavers mainly centered around Arbroath and Dundee. The workers worked independently from home and small workshops called 'manufactories'.

They used small hand looms weaving together the flax into a length of canvas known as a 'bolt'. A bolt was the usually 24" (61cm) in width and about 38 yards (35 metres) long.

Dundee became a centre of excellence in the art of sail-making and fabric manufacture in cotton and linen, becoming known (along with Londonderry in Northern Ireland) as 'Cottonopolis'.

Amazing fact!

It is known that the canvas fore-topsail of HMS Victory was made of Dundee canvas when she sailed into battle against Napoleon's Fleet at Cape Trafalgar in 1805.

To Stretch Or Not To Stretch
That Is The Question

Should thread stretch or not? There are the purists out there who still preach silk for silk, cotton for cotton, nylon for nylon and so on.

These views do not take into account the stunning improvements in technology over the last four decades, especially when it comes to sewing threads. A good quality spun polyester will knock spots of almost any other sewing thread. Do a quick comparison test for yourself. Run two seams along the same fabric and look at the difference. Polyester is stronger, thinner, more flexible, reflects the colour better, slips in-between the warp and weft better and reduces puckering better. In fact it is superior in every way.

Why does your lovely quilt look so puckered? A thousand cotton knots in the fabric, that's why! Why does your dress not move properly? However stretchy your fabric, if you 'lock' it in with a cotton thread, it cannot move.

Some teachers preach that polyester cannot shrink like cotton does, however as it lays into the fabric it gives both ways so even if your cotton quilt does shrink, you should still have a lovely stitch. Industrial manufacturing mainly switched to spun polyester over 30 years ago, giving reliability, durability and flexibility.

Advances in cotton threads have allowed them to improve slightly, but, that has been at the cost of strength. Yes of course sew with a cotton thread but remember for a near perfect stitch nothing beats a good quality modern polyester thread.

When Did Polyester Thread Come Into General Use?

Polyester fabric was invented by two British scientists, James Dickson and John Whinfield, in 1941 and from that point in history some fabrics were made with it. DuPont had the production rights from about 1950.

As polyester gained popularity more and more fabrics and threads were made with it. The great thing with polyester was that it had 'give' in it. This allows the fabric to move with the body. Thread that contained polyester stretched with the seams rather than snap like cotton. It was like a minor miracle, not since the use of silk had a thread performed so well, looked so great AND all at a fraction of the cost!

At first cotton coated polyester came out. However, as polyester proved to be more durable and forgiving, the mix changed from 50-50 to 65-35 and then to 100% polyester.

At Last!
One for all and all for one

In my opinion the finest polyester threads today are made by Gutterman and out-perform cotton threads in every way. Another bonus is that polyester is shiny, so it reflects the fabric it is sewn into. It can be two shades out each way but once in the fabric will look almost a perfect match. Go on try it. Sew a white polyester into a cream fabric and see for yourself.

Threads had come a long way since Coats best six cord cotton. Mind you they have never made better adverts. I love this one, you can even see St Paul's in the London background.

A-HEAD OF ALL OF THEM.

So here we are at the end of our fascinating journey. What started with our early ancestors rolling cotton between their fingers has ended with computers blasting jet air threads through looms at the speed of light, creating endless miles of fabric for our modern world.

Well that's it folks. I hope you've enjoyed our journey through the fascinating world of cotton, threads, spools and so much more.

Bye for now.

The Fascinating World Of Cotton, Threads & Spools
By
Alex Askaroff

Alex Askaroff at Birling Gap

For collectors and enthusiasts
of antique sewing machines and great stories
why not visit

www.sewalot.com

For other publications
by
Alex Askaroff
Visit Amazon

Isaac Singer
The First capitalist
No1 New release

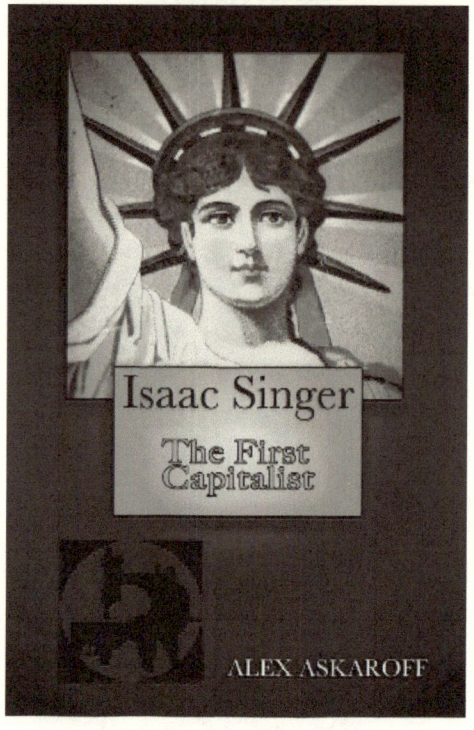

Most of us know the name Singer but few are aware of his amazing life story, his rags to riches journey from a little runaway to one of the richest men of his age. The story of Isaac Merritt Singer will blow your mind, his wives and lovers his castles and palaces, all built on the back of one of the greatest inventions of the 19th century. For the first time the most complete story of a forgotten giant is brought to you by Alex Askaroff.

No1 New Release. No1 Bestseller Amazon certified.

If this isn't the perfect book it's close to it!
I'm on my third run through already.
Love it, love it, love it.
F. Watson USA

Elias Howe
The Man Who Changed The World
No1 New Release Amazon Oct 2019.

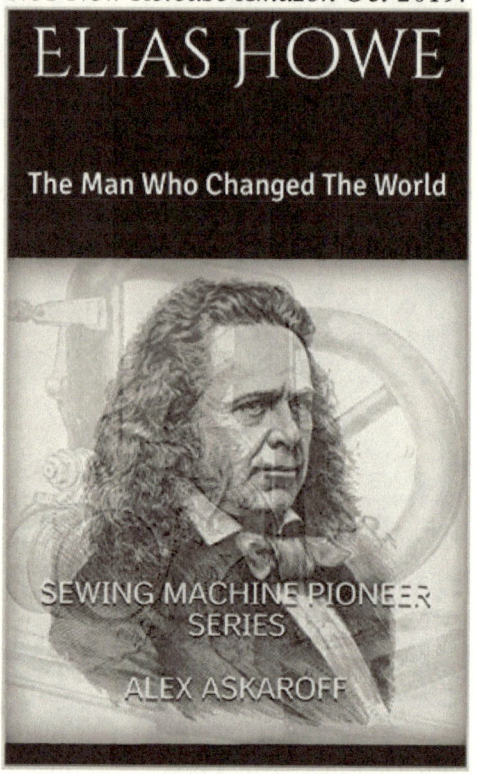

Anyone who uses a sewing machine today has one person to thank, Elias Howe. He was the young farmer with a weak body who figured it out. Elias's life was short and hard, from the largest court cases in legal history to his adventures in the American Civil War. He carved out a name that will live forever. Elias was 48 when he died. In that short time he really was the man who changed the world.

The Luton Hat Trade

THE LUTON HAT TRADE
A Brief History

Alex Askaroff

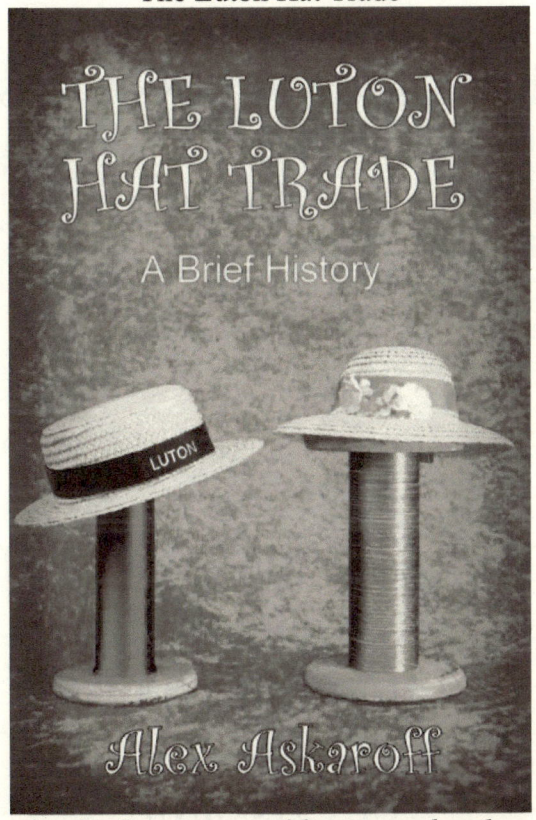

Here for the first time world renowned author Alex Askaroff brings Luton's history back to life with actual stories from hat makers and much more. Come on a journey and discover why some people really were as 'mad as a hatter'.

For other publications
by
Alex Askaroff
visit Amazon

The Fascinating World Of
Cotton,
Threads & Spools
By
Alex Askaroff

On The Road Series

*Alex has over 30 books on Amazon with Eight No1 New Releases. There are seven books in Alex Askaroff's **On The Road Series**. They cover his working life around Sussex, encompassing a world of stories from the ages.*

Book One: Patches of Heaven

Book Two: Skylark Country

Book Three: High Streets & Hedgerows

Book Four: Tales From The Coast

Book Five: Have I Got A Story For You

Book Six: Glory Days

Book Seven: Off The Beaten Track

A few of my favourite remarks about my books (amazingly there are another 30 pages of them on my Sewalot.com website received from all over the globe.)

You'll be back for more – Country Life

Evocative and descriptive. Excellent writing – Professor Jacque Johnson

Wonderful warm and charming. Alex has a remarkable talent – Anne Brennan: President Allegro Communications.

Alex's books are rare, desired and most welcome – Capt R. Wightman

A trilogy of local gems – Aspect County Magazine. You will be entranced by his stories and travels around Sussex – Sussex Books.

A well-polished masterpiece – What's On Magazine

You may feel that you know Sussex but I guarantee Alex will make you look again and fill your minds with the happiest of thoughts – Frank Scutt OBE

I retired to my bed, and let your book give me a glimpse of somewhere else, through the eyes of someone else. By the time I turned off my reading light, I was at peace with the world, not convinced it is either safe or sane, but the edge softened by your beautiful words. – Pat Bergman, USA

I couldn't put it down, Hillaire Belloc would have been happy to put his name to a book like this –
John Allen, Magnet Magazine

Word pictures of landscapes and pictures straight from the heart. A fascinating read – Jim Flegg, Country Ways Television

Full of laughter, even a few tears, folklore and wisdom. Books to be dipped into and treasured a delightful trilogy – The Hash

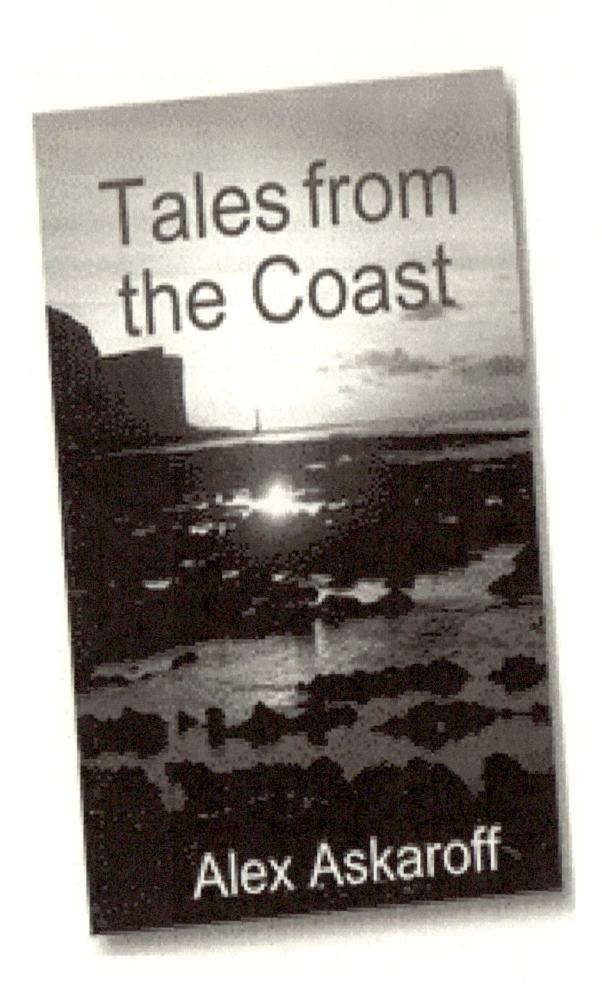

Tales from the Coast, Book Four in Alex's On The Road Series, continues the true stories which he brings both England's history and people vividly to life. The stories are as pleasurable as a warm bath after a long day. From the disappearance of Lord Lucan in Uckfield to the Buxted Witch, from William Duke of Normandy to Queen Elizabeth's Eastbourne dressmaker, Tales from the Coast is crammed with a fascinating mix of true stories that will have you entranced from start to finish.

*Yet again Alex has woven his magic. I kept saying I
never knew that and I'm a local. This may just be
one of the best books I've ever read!
J. Vincent*

Alex, I've read every book James Herriot ever wrote, and my favorite topics in his books are about the animals and the meals, just like my favorite stories in your books are the ones that talk about your experiences working in people's homes. I love them. Thank you so much.
Joe Edmiston
Louisville, KY

Alex Askaroff has had Eight No1 New Releases on Amazon. For decades Alex has been enthralling readers around the world with his writing. Off The Beaten Track is the seventh book in his On The Road Series.

www.sewalot.com
My antique sewing machine site.

Sir Sewalot, protector of Sewalot.com